C000157206

LONDON
PAST AND PRESENT

LONDON
PAST AND PRESENT

MICHAEL BARRETT
AND DOUGLAS WHITWORTH

TEMPUS

ACKNOWLEDGEMENTS

I would like to thank the following for their much valued help: Canary Wharf Press Office; Coin Street Community Builders; Dockland's Light Railway Press Office; London City Airport Press Office; Metropolitan Police Museum; Royal Festival Hall Press Office; Wandsworth Riverside Waste Authority.

I would also like to thank Margaret and Douglas Whitworth for their kind help and encouragement.

Above: At the end of the Thames Festival, an annual event hosted by the Mayor of London, tens of thousands of people are thrilled at the sights and sounds of the fireworks. The fireworks are fired from a barge positioned mid-stream in the River Thames between Waterloo and Blackfriars Bridges.

Frontispiece: Monument sculpted by John W. Mills ARCA FRBS in honour and memory of those firefighters who gave their lives in the defence of the nation in 1939-1945.

First published 2007

Tempus Publishing Ltd
The Mill, Brimscombe Port
Stroud, Gloucestershire GL5 2QG
www.tempus-publishing.com

© Michael Barrett and Douglas Whitworth, 2007

The right of Michael Barrett and Douglas Whitworth to be identified as the Authors of this work has been asserted by them in accordance with the Copyrights, Designs and Patents Act 1988.

All rights reserved. No part of this book may be reprinted or reproduced or utilised in any form or by any electronic, mechanical or other means, now known or hereafter invented, including photocopying and recording, or in any information storage or retrieval system, without the permission in writing from the Publishers.

British Library Cataloguing in Publication Data.
A catalogue record for this book is available from the British Library.

ISBN 978 0 7524 4304 1

Typesetting, design and origination by Tempus Publishing.
Printed in Great Britain

INTRODUCTION

In 2006 my abiding interest in the history of London led me to purchase *London – Life in the Post-War Years* with Douglas Whitworth's striking photographs of London in the 1940s and 1950s.

These photographs were particularly evocative in recapturing the London of my student days, living in the then unfashionable Notting Hill Gate. So, book in hand I sought to identify the locations of Douglas' photographs. Of course, fifty or so years later the city had changed, but not beyond recognition. One by one I located Douglas' original camera positions and soon decided to take my camera along to mark the changes which were in some cases, too slight to be worth recording. Other locations were impossible to shoot from exactly the same camera position, obscured now by mature trees that in Douglas' photographs appeared as recently planted saplings, some from a viewpoint now far too dangerous due to the traffic maelstrom of a 1960s multi-lane road system.

Quite early in the exercise it became obvious it would be counter-productive to slavishly seek out the same camera positions as the original photographs. A case in point was the shot from Waterloo Bridge towards Somerset House. In the intervening fifty years there appeared to have been no substantial change to the view. However, by moving back 20m or so, significant changes were revealed – now a cycle lane and signs directing traffic through the Kingsway tunnel appear in the foreground.

With my 2006 photographs I have endeavoured to illustrate some of the major changes to the fabric and environment of London and its citizens – many of my photographs illustrate a direct contrast to Douglas' images of fifty years ago. However, some of the more recent changes – the Canary Wharf development and the Thames Barrier – 'stand on their own'. I have chosen a few examples.

Fifty years ago at Buckingham Palace, one of my earliest revisited locations, the majority of overseas visitors were from the USA. Now, visitors 'from across the pond' are outnumbered by tourists from the other side of the world to the East, who come equipped to take home a digital image of Royal Britain.

In the early post-war years no stigma was attached to hopping on a bus or diving down the tube, it was a pleasure to travel on a London bus with one of those conductors whose aim in life was to run a happy ship. Traffic was minimal, car ownership was not yet seen as an inalienable right and there were few on the roads. For those who had them, often running on tyres with rubber run down to the canvas, parking in the street at their place of work or, for an afternoon's shopping outside a West End department store – was accepted as the norm and would excite no police attention. However, as the decades passed and the number of journeys into central London by private-car grew and the hell of rush hour soon extended to all-day misery, gridlock became reality. Various traffic management schemes were tried. One-way streets and circulatory systems were introduced – a major one at Hyde Park Corner. Entering the traffic flow from Piccadilly was once described to me by a cabby as 'sorting the men from the boys'. In 1959 yellow lines were painted on roads and parking meters introduced with traffic wardens to police them a year later. Alas, all proved to be 'sticking plaster' measures. Finally a Congestion Zone, encompassing the majority of West End and city streets, was introduced. Any vehicle entering the zone (Monday to Friday) attracted a charge of £5 per day (now increased to £8 per day). This now encompasses a much wider exclusion zone with threats of even higher charges for 'gas-guzzlers'.

Walking through the streets of Mayfair on my photographic expedition I was taken aback by the number of empty parking meter bays. Once the subject of heated disputes between drivers competing for an hour's ownership – the majority are now unoccupied, their meters used as hitching posts by the thousands of commuters' pedal cycles. I photographed one.

St Paul's remained the tallest building in the city until the late 1950s when a building's maximum height was limited by law to 100ft. With the relaxation of this law, developers of mainly commercial buildings, increased their valuable square footage available for rental by building ever higher.

Opened in 1965, the Post Office Tower, at 620ft, was by far London's tallest structure. The NatWest Tower now renamed Tower 42 (opened by the Queen in 1981) was at 600ft – 42 storeys – the highest building in Europe. It lost its place as the tallest building in London to Canary Wharf's One Canada Square (50 storeys) in 1991. Even higher office blocks are planned. Though not a skyscraper, the latest and most celebrated office building is the Swiss Re Tower, affectionately known as the 'Gherkin'.

Following the closure of the loss-making PLA West India and Millwall Docks between 1978 and 1980, the Docklands Development Corporation

was created to secure regeneration by stimulating industry and commerce. People were encouraged to live and work in the area by providing housing and social facilities. In 1991 the first tenants moved into the developer's flagship project, the Canary Wharf Tower. With the resurgence of confidence after a period of severe recession, work started on the HSBC and City Group towers which were ready for occupation in late 2001.

For the successful development of the London Docklands good communications were essential. The Docklands Light Railway (DLR) linked Canary Wharf with the City of London. Operation started in 1987 with eleven trains running on ten miles of track. Later an extension to Bank underground was built and now ninety-three driverless trains run on twenty miles of track. An additional extension of track to Woolwich Arsenal is due to open in 2009 and Stratford International, an interchange station with Eurostar trains in 2010.

In 1987 the first scheduled flights using STOL (Short Takeoff and Landing) took off from London City Airport, using a runway constructed on Heron Quay, the long quay between the two recently closed Royal Group of Docks. Year by year aircraft movements increased – partly due to the introduction of the faster pure jet aircraft in 1992. In 2005 over 70,000 aircraft movements, operating from this 1,319m runway, carried over 2 million passengers to destinations in the UK and Europe. Many passengers descend by escalator, from DLR to London City Airport station (opened in December 2005, by London's Mayor Ken Livingstone) directly to the departure hall.

After the catastrophic floods of 1953 it became apparent that a comprehensive flood strategy was needed. In addition to raising the banks of the Thames in vulnerable areas, a flood barrier would be essential. Alternative solutions were investigated but the design adopted, a series of ten separate rising gates supported between concrete tiers, sited across the Thames at Woolwich, gained Royal Assent in 1972. Work began in 1974 and on 8 May 1984 I had the pleasure of filming the ceremony when the Queen declared the barrier neither open nor closed, but 'operational'. Since then the barrier has been deployed many more times than projected each year.

At this point I must pay tribute to the creative and technical skill of Douglas Whitworth. Using cameras with none of the automatic features we now take for granted, shooting on 'slow' black and white film and finally, in his darkroom, creating these evocative images.

During my revisiting London exercise I enjoyed, once again, taking a 'stills' camera to photograph parts of London which fifty-plus years ago, often lacking the bus fare, I explored on foot and hope you will enjoy this pictorial journey.

Michael Barrett, 2007

Opposite page: St Mary-le-Bow church with its porch and tower standing aside from the gutted nave in 1953. The bells of the church, which called Dick Whittington to turn again, have been famous since 1091. The present steeple built by Sir Christopher Wren is considered to be his masterpiece and not since the 1960s, when the area surrounding it was rebuilt, has it been possible to appreciate its full glory. The church was restored by Laurence King between 1956 and 1972 by which time new office building has ensured that unrestricted views of the church were a thing of the past. (Douglas Whitworth)

Below: Looking east, the view with St Mary-le-Bow, centre frame, shows the most dramatic transformation of all the Stone Gallery views.

The scene is dominated by the two tallest towers in the city: Tower 42 (formerly the NatWest Tower) and the Swiss Re Tower. Most of the Victorian offices have been modernised. Others, behind their preserved, original façade, substantially rebuilt and of course, every square foot of land previously used as bomb site car parks, has been developed into valuable commercial real estate.

THE TRAITORS' GATE

Left: Looking east two buildings stand out. Though affectionately known as the Gherkin this innovative design by Lord Foster is less well known by its correct title the Swiss Re building. At 30 St Mary Axe this 41-storey office is London's second highest building,

Opposite above left: The view towards London's river and Westminster from the Stone Gallery of St Paul's Cathedral in 1953. Hemmed in by the huddle of warehouses and offices is the square tower of St Andrew-by-the-Wardrobe, gutted during the Second World War but later restored. By the river is the huge curved frontage of Unilever House built in 1930-1932 on the site of Royal Hotel. Beyond the River Thames is the waterfront of Southwark and in the distance, the towers of Westminster. (Douglas Whitworth)

Opposite above right: Unilever House looks outwardly the same, though cleaned and restored. On the South Bank, just upstream, is the Oxo building, celebrating the tenth anniversary of its rebirth as a centre for specialist shops, artists' and designers' studios. On the eighth floor, boasting panoramic views of the river and St Paul's, is the exclusive Oxo Tower Restaurant.

The neighbouring Sea Containers House and behind, the International Publishing Corporation building, combine to overshadow the Oxo Tower. Further upstream, the London Eye is partially obscured by a tower block, built as London Weekend's Television Centre. Now the offices and studios are used by several independent television companies. Beyond, the green roof of the Royal Festival Hall can be seen amongst the foliage of, now, mature trees, planted in 1951 as part of the Festival of Britain.

Above: Ludgate Hill from St Paul's in 1948. The slender spire on the right of the street is St Martin Ludgate, the city church that suffered least damage of any during the war. At the bottom of the hill, the tallest of all Sir Christopher Wren's churches is St Bride's, apparently unscathed but in fact only a shell. The north tower of St Paul's on the right was originally intended to have a clock similar to the one in the south tower, but it was never installed. (Douglas Whitworth)

Right: In the distance, to the right of St Paul's Tower, is the Post Office Tower (now the BT Tower) for many years the tallest building in London.

Left: In the early eighteenth century St George's Bloomsbury, consecrated in 1731, was the last of six churches designed by Nicholas Hawksmoor, built to accommodate the respectable residents of the parish of St Giles-in-the-Fields. They objected to having to pass through the notorious district known as the 'Rookery' (scene of Hogarth's *Gin Lane*) in order to attend church.

As recently as 2003 St George's was on the Buildings at Risk register, but generous grants by, amongst others, The Paul Mellon Foundation and the Heritage Lottery Fund made it possible for extensive restoration work to begin. On 5 October 2006 HRH Prince Michael of Kent GCVO attended a service of thanksgiving for the restoration of the church.

The extraordinary steeple is stepped like a pyramid with lions and unicorns at its base carved by Tim Crawley, the originals having been removed as unsafe during the last restoration in 1870. The portico, based on the Temple of Bacchus of Baalbec in the Lebanon, is considered to be the most handsome Georgian portico in London.

Below: 1948 – St Paul's Cathedral from Fleet Street. The view up Ludgate Hill was spoilt by the nineteenth-century railway viaduct then spanning the road, but beyond is the slender spire of St Martin Ludgate contrasting with the great dome of St Paul's. (Douglas Whitworth)

The railway viaduct has gone, allowing a closer view of this – Wren's great design. Though Wren's initial plans were submitted in 1669, the building work was not completed until 1710. As part of the 300th anniversary restoration the west façade has had 300 years of grime removed. Now, viewed by light filtered through a yet-to-be-dispersed early morning mist, produces a pleasing image of this, London's architectural Jewel in the Crown.

Some dates in the cathedral's history worthy of mention:

1806   Funeral service for Admiral Lord Nelson

1940   Cathedral firebombed

1965   Funeral service of Sir Winston Churchill

1981   The marriage of Charles, Prince of Wales to Lady Diana Spencer

I was pleased to include in my shot the two cyclists turning right into Ludgate Hill. In Douglas' early post-war photographs, cycle ownership was generally seen as being limited to blue-collar workers, schoolteachers and district nurses and certainly not as a suitable image for successful business executives, who would drive to city offices in their Humber or Jaguar saloons. Now thousands of city workers of all grades have adopted pedal power as part of their fitness regime. Many companies, recognising this transport revolution, have installed showers and changing facilities. Some even supply company cycles.

Above left: Newspaper offices in Fleet Street, 1949. The great twentieth-century offices of the *Daily Telegraph* and the *Daily Express* stand out from the older buildings, mainly occupied by the provincial newspapers and agencies. Intermingled with the great newspaper offices were the innumerable cafés and bars, frequented by journalists and printers. Bars such as Yates's, Mooney's and El Vino's had their regular patrons who rarely strayed from them.

On the left down Wine Office Court is the Old Cheshire Cheese dating from 1667, a haunt of Dr Samuel Johnson. Adjoining it is the Queen of Scots House built in 1905 with a statue of Mary Stuart in an alcove on the front, with next to it, the King and Keys – a public house favoured by journalists of the *Daily Telegraph* – tourists tended to frequent Lyons' or ABC cafés. (Douglas Whitworth)

Above right: The first newspaper to open a Fleet Street office was the *Daily Courant*, in 1702. Over the years it became the centre of newspaper publishing until in 1986, when despite huge print union antipathy, *News International* transferred its offices and production facilities to Wapping. Other newspapers followed suit and the last to leave was the world-renowned news agency Reuters.

Right: Gone are the traffic jams caused by the lorries as they manoeuvred their huge rolls of newsprint, and taxis carrying journalists and photographers returning with 'hot' stories no longer stop at newspaper offices. Happily, the façades of the newspaper offices have been restored. I was pleased to be able to photograph the Art Deco detail that has been retained.

Right: In the interest of research I investigated the hostelries mentioned by Douglas. Though the ABC and Lyons' cafés are long gone, El Vino remains. Once the favourite venue for PR executives seeking to enthuse a journalist with their corporate client's latest press release, they no longer throng the 'gentlemen only' bar and are now tied to their office desks where communication is electronic.

Below: I like to think that Ye Olde Cheshire Cheese remains much the same as when one of Dr Johnson's favourite watering holes. Seated under the doctor's portrait, I met a group of retired print workers who, together with their wives, meet regularly to swap stories of their working lives in 'the street'.

Though all the newspaper offices have gone, Wren's church, St Bride's, remains the printers' and journalists' church.

Queen Victoria Street and the River Thames from St Paul's in 1948. The Wren church of St Nicholas Cole Abbey on the left, burnt out and missing its spire, has since been restored and is now used by the Free Church of Scotland. Beyond in Upper Thames Street is the tower of St Mary Somerset which was saved from destruction in 1869 when the rest of the church was pulled down. The Blitz of the Second World War gave the authorities the same opportunity to replan the city as had been given to the architects of the seventeenth century after the Great Fire of London. In the event, none of the proposed reconstruction plans were realised. (Douglas Whitworth)

The two churches Douglas photographed in 1948, are just visible among the temples to Mammon, but look to the west where a line has been drawn to further office development and an avenue created from St Paul's leading to the river and beyond, to Tate Modern, via the Millennium Bridge. The line of ants in my photograph are visitors crossing the bridge.

Designed by Sir Norman Foster, the 320m-long bridge is sometimes described as a 'blade of light'.

When it opened on 10 June 2000 some 80,000 people crossed the bridge and it soon became apparent that it had developed an alarming wobble; it was closed three days later. In January 2002 before the public were once again allowed the crossing from St Paul's to Tate Modern or the Globe Theatre, the modifications made to the bridge were tested by 2,000 people, led by the Mayor of Southwark, marching across the bridge. Following this success, the Millennium Bridge was finally reopened in February 2002.

Top left: Designed by Sir Giles Gilbert Scott and first commissioned as Bankside Power Station in 1963, it has, unlike the four chimneys of his Battersea Power Station only one 99m-high central chimney. Though closed in 1981 and at one point listed for demolition, it was reborn (in May 2000) as the Tate Modern, a gallery celebrating contemporary art. The huge 35 metre-high Turbine Hall now hosts works by internationally recognised modern artists. The Tate and Tate Modern are linked by a regular riverboat service.

Middle left: On a summer's evening, the Millennium Bridge is still busy with visitors enjoying the magic of London's riverside views. Some are making their way to and from a monumental though featureless brick building distinctive by its tall central chimney.

Bottom left: A performance is under way at the Globe Theatre; the audience either sit in the circular gallery, or stand (Groundlings) as did audiences of 400 years ago. This is thanks to the American actor Sam Wannamaker who founded the Shakespeare Globe Trust and persevered for over twenty years to recreate Shakespeare's Globe on its original site. Sadly he never lived to see a production staged in his Elizabethan theatre as he died some years before it was opened by HM The Queen in 1997.

Top right: Late evening and a few stragglers still cross the Millennium Bridge. Downstream illuminated after dark, Southwark Bridge and Tower Bridge look even better than by day (London Bridge is obscured by Southwark Bridge).

Bottom right: Visitors to Tate Modern cross the Millennium Bridge. To the north is an almost uninterrupted view of St Paul's Cathedral.

Above left: The outlines in 1948 of the warehouses and offices that lined Cannon Street before the Blitz of 29 December 1940. This was the worst air raid of the war on London to that date and although the surrounding streets were devastated, St Paul's, by a miracle, was saved. At the bottom left is Anderson's rubber warehouse and beyond is the square burnt-out tower of St Augustine Watling Street which has now been restored and incorporated into St Paul's Cathedral Choir School. Reconstruction of this area was not to begin for several years and many bombed sites were used as temporary car parks. (Douglas Whitworth)

Above right: The devastated landscape of Douglas' 1948 photograph must have looked very similar to that of 1666 after the Great Fire. An example of this is the large building in the left middle distance which was built on the site of offices destroyed in the war which, in turn, was built on the site of the church of St John and destroyed by the Great Fire. Then as now, trade fuelled property development, businesses 'bombed out' returned and the advantage of a 'City' address attracted new companies.

Below left: The Pool of London from the Monument in 1948, with a ship preparing to sail under Tower Bridge. The roof and front of Billingsgate Market is on the immediate right – in the early morning the market and surrounding streets would be full of porters and traders carrying boxes of all varieties of fish. Long considered a nuisance in this position, the market was transferred to the Isle of Dogs in 1982. In the centre foreground is the Coal Exchange, demolished in 1962 for road widening and beyond, with its long river frontage, is the Custom House. In the left background is the White Tower of the Tower of London. (Douglas Whitworth)

Below right: To include HMS *Belfast* and the Tower of London's White Tower, this is slightly wider than Douglas' shot. Centre frame, Tower Bridge lifts to allow the 60m-long brig *Prince William* to pass upstream to berth alongside HMS *Belfast*. In the foreground Billingsgate Market, after a successful conversion to office space, remains unoccupied. On the South Bank and upstream from Tower Bridge, replacing the cranes and wharves, is City Hall.

Above: This striking new landmark on the Thames, City Hall, from 2002 home to the Mayor of London, was designed by Foster & Partners to be an energy-efficient and environmentally friendly building. In the foreground, the land surrounding City Hall is being landscaped and will shortly be opened as a public space.

Far right: HMS *Belfast*, built in 1939, the largest British cruiser at 11,000 tons, saw service during the Second World War including a major supporting role on the D-Day landings. After her final exercise in the Mediterranean she was paid off in 1963. Happily she was saved from the scrapyard and brought to her present berth and opened to the public on Trafalgar Day 1971.

Right: The 60m brig *Prince William*, lying alongside HMS *Belfast*, was built in 2001 as a sail training ship for the Tall Ships Youth Trust. Crewed by six permanent members and forty-eight young trainees from ten countries, she set sail from Brixham, bound for London, arriving ten days later.

Above: The skyline from Waterloo Bridge in 1953 before office blocks and towers rose to compete with St Paul's for dominance. Moored by the Victoria Embankment, from the left are Captain Scott's *Discovery*, HQS *Wellington* and HMS *President* and *Chrysanthemum*. The latter two ships which saw service in the First World War were converted into headquarters and training ships of the Royal Naval Volunteer Reserve. The *Chrysanthemum* has been scrapped but the *President* is now the headquarters of Inter-Action, an educational trust. The wedding cake spire of St Bride's is visible in the centre of the picture – the only part of the church remaining after an air raid in 1940. (Douglas Whitworth)

Left: The dome of St Paul's and the spire of St Bride's no longer dominate the skyline, dwarfed by Tower 42 and the Swiss Re Tower. Captain Scott's *Discovery* at Temple Pier has been replaced by several craft trading as floating bars, restaurants and a nightclub. The large modern building beyond Temple Pier is the headquarters of British American Tobacco. The craft in the foreground is a Thames Clipper, a high-speed catamaran operating a commuter service between Central London, Canary Wharf and Greenwich.

Above: The south bank of the River Thames in 1953. The Festival of Britain held in 1951 transformed this previously derelict area into an eye-catching exhibition centre. The Royal Festival Hall on the extreme left was the only building intended to be permanent and the river bank between Waterloo Bridge and Hungerford Railway Bridge was laid out as a promenade. Beyond the railway bridge, which is now having new footbridges built on each side, are the government buildings on Victoria Embankment and the Victorian Gothic Palace of Westminster. (Douglas Whitworth)

Right: Now, over fifty years later, the mature trees planted for the Festival of Britain made it impossible to photograph the South Bank from the same viewpoint as Douglas' 1953 shot. The most obvious addition to the scene is the London Eye, a 135m observation wheel. Less obvious is the downstream Jubilee Bridge, one of two pedestrian bridges built either side of Hungerford Railway Bridge, a popular crossing point for visitors heading for the South Bank Arts Complex.

Top left: The Royal Festival Hall and the Shot Tower from Victoria Embankment in 1951. The South Bank Exhibition was created on a 27-acre site, derelict since the end of the war, and was the beginning of the development of an arts centre on the south side of the Thames. The Shot Tower as well as being open to the public carried scientific apparatus to record radio signals from outer space. (Douglas Whitworth)

Middle left: As the first phase of a major redevelopment of the South Bank Arts Complex, the Royal Festival Hall is closed to the public until mid-2007. The Grade 1 Listed building is being restored and refurbished in keeping with its original 1950s design. By summer 2005 the refurbishment and landscaping of the ground floor on the river front was completed. Meanwhile, work to improve audience comfort, access for people with disabilities and concert hall acoustics was carried out. A later phase includes work to landscape the area surrounding the Royal Festival Hall, Queens Walk and to completely transform Jubilee Gardens into a public space of outstanding beauty.

Bottom left: The Royal Festival Hall under construction in 1950. This was the first concert hall to be built in London after the war and was the only permanent structure of the Festival of Britain South Bank Exhibition. The festival, held throughout the summer of 1951, was conceived as a celebration of recovery from the war and to mark the centenary of the Great Exhibition held in Hyde Park. The Surrey Shot Tower on the left was used as a beacon during the festival. (Douglas Whitworth)

Below: The Grade 1 Listed fifty-five-year-old Festival Hall is undergoing a £91 million refurbishment and will be closed to the public until the concert hall reopens for performances in June 2007. While the river front exterior of the hall and terrace undergoes a substantial restoration and remodelling, the major part of the work to the interior is to improve the acoustics of the concert hall.

Below right: In spite of their mother's entreaties, three young boys gambol as jets of water shoot up outside the Festival Hall. The fountains on this site are temporary and will be replaced on a regular basis by those of other designers. In the background – you've guessed it!

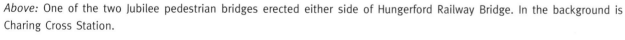

Above: One of the two Jubilee pedestrian bridges erected either side of Hungerford Railway Bridge. In the background is Charing Cross Station.

Top right: The London Eye remains one of London's premier tourist attractions and has revitalised the South Bank.

Middle right: Visitors in their glass pod commencing a half-hour 'flight' and anticipating the enjoyment of panoramic views over London as they climb to a height of 135m.

Bottom right: Across the Thames is Westminster Pier, the busiest of cruise boat piers. Beyond is the recently opened Portcullis House with five floors of offices for MPs which has an underground tunnel leading directly to the Palace of Westminster.

Left: The Festival of Britain Exhibition from Westminster Bridge, 1951. The festival was a tonic to the nation after the long years of war and the years of austerity that had followed it. The South Bank Exhibition was not only a trade fair but an informative and enjoyable day out for the family. (Douglas Whitworth)

Below: No longer the home to London's governing council, this imposing building has been converted into a complex of apartments, two hotels, restaurants and a health and leisure club. It also houses the London Aquarium and a permanent Dali exhibition.

Erected on the nearby Jubilee Gardens and first operational in January 2000, the London Eye, a 135m-diameter observation wheel is an attractive new addition to the London skyline. During a half-hour flight (the London Eye is operated by British Airways) visitors enjoy panoramic views across London and on a clear day, twenty-five miles away Windsor Castle.

Far right: The Clock Tower of the Houses of Parliament, known as Big Ben, certainly the best-known sight of London. The perfectly proportioned tower balances the taller Victoria Tower to the south. Parliament Square is still an oasis surrounded by rushing traffic with many statues of great statesmen on the lawns. (Douglas Whitworth)

Above right: On a bright but chilly winter's afternoon, visitors to London pose for a photograph in front of London's best-known landmark. On the left is the statue of Jan Christian Smuts, and in the middle distance Winston Churchill by Ivor Roberts-Jones. In the far distance is Portcullis House.

Below right: At a ceremony in February 2001 the Queen opened Portcullis House. Built to house 310 MPs and their staff with its bombproof walls and windows, it is Britain's most expensive office block.

Left: This is the television crews' chosen location for a political story or when interviewing politicians fresh from a lively debate across the road. The afternoon I took this photograph there were five news crews at work.

Below left: The grass in the foreground of this shot of the Victoria Tower is testament to the long drought suffered by the United Kingdom in 2005/06.

Opposite above left: Trams on Victoria Embankment in 1950, two years before the last tram ran in central London. The first electric trams in London were run by Clifton Robinson in 1901, followed in 1903 by the London County Council, but it was not until 1906 that permission was given for trams to run along Victoria Embankment and over Westminster Bridge. In the 1930s the replacement of trams by trolley buses began and this well-loved form of transport began to disappear from the streets of London. Almost half a century later in 1999, a modern tram system was inaugurated in Croydon. (Douglas Whitworth)

Opposite above right: Now open-top buses cruise along the Victoria Embankment conducted by English-speaking guides, with an additional recorded commentary in other languages. Part of this popular tour takes the bus along the north side of the Thames towards the Houses of Parliament. Other themed tours are available.

Opposite below left: British Railways Standard 4-6-2 Britannia class Pacific No. 70004 *William Shakespeare* locomotive, which headed the Golden Arrow train leaving Victoria Railway Station for Dover in 1953. This locomotive had been on display at the South Bank Exhibition of the Festival of Britain in 1951, before being introduced into service with the Southern Region later in the year. Holidays abroad were still a rarity for the average Briton and those who made the crossing to the continent were restricted to a £25 travel allowance. The glamour of this train and the opulence of the first-class compartments were equal to the Orient Express in Europe. (Douglas Whitworth)

Opposite below right: A Eurostar train leaving its dedicated platform at Waterloo Station en route for the Gare du Nord in Paris. Though lacking the glamour and first-class service one would expect of the Golden Arrow, travel by Eurostar allows one to take a late breakfast in London and later that same day, enjoy lunch in the centre of Paris. Eurostar has been operating its London to Paris service since 1994 when Queen Elizabeth and President Mitterrand performed the opening ceremonies in both Calais and Folkestone. Eurostar's Waterloo terminal will close later in 2007 when its service will be extended to St Pancras Station where new platforms are being built.

Left: The British Overseas Airways Corporation (BOAC) headquarters on Buckingham Palace Road, 1949. The building was constructed in 1939 for Imperial Airways, the predecessor of BOAC. (Douglas Whitworth)

Above left: A Docklands Light Railway train draws into London City Airport station. Operations started in 1987, with eleven trains on ten miles of track.

Above right: Later an extension to Bank underground interchange station was built. Now ninety-three driverless trains run on twenty miles of track. The London City Airport Station was opened in December 2005, by London's Mayor Ken Livingstone with an additional extension of track due to reach Woolwich Arsenal in 2009, and Stratford International, an interchange station with Eurostar trains in 2010.

The sleek de Havilland Comet airliner taking off from Heathrow for Johannesburg in 1953. Flights commenced in May 1952 inaugurating the world's first jet plane passenger service. In 1954 a Comet crashed into the sea shortly after taking off from Rome. Metal fatigue was judged to be the cause of the crash which effectively ended the airliner's life for commercial transport. (Douglas Whitworth)

Flight LX445, bound for Geneva, climbs out past London City Airport's control tower. At Heathrow Airport in 1982, aircraft landed every two minutes or so. Across London, in June that year, a lone Dash 7 STOL (Short Takeoff and Landing) aircraft touched down, safely, on the long quay between the two recently closed Royal Group of Docks. This flight demonstrated the feasibility of Heron Quay as the runway of an STOL port.

In 1986 after planning permission was granted, Prince Charles laid the foundation stone of the terminal building and in October the following year, the first commercial flight took off from London City Airport's runway 10.

In 2005 over 70,000 aircraft movements operating from this 1,319m runway carried close on 2 million passengers to destinations in UK and Europe. Many passengers descend by escalator from the London City Airport station, directly to the departure hall.

Although Heathrow, the world's busiest airport would have been the obvious choice for an update of Douglas' Comet photograph, I decided to concentrate my efforts on the comparatively tiny London City Airport where departing aircraft, Control Tower and Terminal Building can be included as one image.

Top right: Traffic on the ring road of Hyde Park near Stanhope Gate in 1949, heavy then as now, with a policeman on the road attempting to control the flow of cars. (Douglas Whitworth)

Top far right: The Cumberland Hotel, Marble Arch, 1949. The hotel and adjoining Lyons Corner House attracted many tourists and businessmen. The Cumberland has eight floors below ground level – these were invaluable during the war when they were used as air-raid shelters. In the foreground is a 12-horsepower Austin low-loader taxicab, already superseded by the Austin FX3, introduced in 1948 and destined to become London's 'black cab'. (Douglas Whitworth)

Middle: The Cumberland Hotel at Marble Arch in 1949. The Cumberland, which was opened in 1933, was the first hotel in London with 1,000 rooms, each with an adjoining bathroom. The hotel was built to attract American tourists and businessmen and from its opening was equipped with soda fountains and air-conditioning. The rooms were all fitted to a high standard and were then 22s for a single and 36s 6d for a double room. The Marble Arch on the left was originally erected in front of Buckingham Palace but was transferred to its present site for the Great Exhibition of 1851 and stood as the original entrance to Hyde Park. (Douglas Whitworth)

Bottom: Following the introduction of the Park Lane one-way system there have been some changes in traffic flow. However, Marble Arch remains the centre of a one-way traffic system, only accessed by pedestrians via some rather scary tunnels.

In the foreground is a 'Bendy Bus', also known by some as the 'free bus' since entry can be made, quite correctly, by a door to the rear, well away and out of sight of the driver – the unscrupulous travel without paying. At 18m long and carrying up to 140 passengers, 130 of these Mercedes-built buses are currently on trial in London. After an inauspicious start (one burst into flames in Park Lane) they are not universally popular. The Oxford Street façade of the Cumberland Hotel is largely unchanged, though each of the 1,000 bedrooms has been upgraded over the years. Now each room has a large-screen television entertainment centre and a connection to the Internet. The 1949 room rate has increased substantially – I was quoted, in 2006, from £150 to £200 per night B&B.

Above left: The final evolution of London Transport's Design Department, the Routemaster bus first took to the streets in the mid-1950s and was gone by 2005. Reproduced on greeting cards and tourist guides it was by far the most popular symbol of our metropolis. Though the last Routemaster bus as a major public transport vehicle was withdrawn from service in December 2005, a small number continue in service on two short 'heritage' routes. Visitors to London may experience the now unique and final opportunity of buying their ticket from a bus conductor. I photographed this No. 9 passing the Albert Memorial, the last stop on its route.

Above right: On the No. 15 route, this Routemaster is passing what was, in the heyday of the London Docks, the Port of London Authority Building.

Left: The American Embassy in Grosvenor Square, 1949. This was built in 1937 but in the 1950s a massive new embassy with a 999-year lease was constructed on the west side of the square which had been heavily bombed during the war. Throughout the conflict the lovely garden in the centre of the square was turned to practical use when a crew of the Women's Auxiliary Air Force manned a barrage balloon here – they named it Romeo! The cars in front of the embassy are both American, a Cadillac on the left and a Packard on the right. (Douglas Whitworth)

Below left: Leaving its modest home at No. 1 Grosvenor Square in 1960, the American Embassy moved to a large purpose-designed embassy building occupying the entire west side of the square. After the 9/11 terrorist attacks large concrete blocks appeared in streets on three sides of the embassy. All traffic is now completely excluded from the west side of Grosvenor Square.

Below right: The statue of General Dwight D. Eisenhower stands on the north side of the embassy, observed by the unblinking eye of the security cameras. He seems to be gazing at a curious relic from the past – an ancient, blue Metropolitan Police Post. Though taken out of service in the 1970s it remains as an item of historical interest.

Bottom left: An American Oldsmobile with gleaming chrome in Grosvenor Square, 1948. In the background are the offices of Way & Waller, one of London's pre-eminent estate agents. The early period after the war was a time when many great houses of Mayfair were empty, either due to bomb damage or because their owners now found them too expensive to run. Many were sold and replaced by modern buildings. (Douglas Whitworth)

Left: The nation's most prestigious car, choice of royalty, the Rolls Royce, gazes out through the plate-glass window of its Berkeley Square showroom, to the petite-newcomer to London streets, the G-Wiz all-electric car. There are lots of benefits for its owner: the £8 charge to enter the Capital's Congestion Zone is waived; it costs a miserly one penny a mile; and finally, parking meter bays come free of charge.

Below: The only way in the twenty-first century for the bride-to-be and her friends to start the night in style: quaffing champagne while relaxing in the back of a pink stretch limo en route to a club catering for hen-night revels.

Above: This cyclist is one of a large group of cycle messengers operating in the West End and the City. His cycle is stripped down to virtually a frame and two wheels.

Right: A comparatively recent sight in the West End is the large number of cycle rickshaws plying for hire – most appear only in the evening. With no current regulation the fare, for a maximum of two passengers, is subject to negotiation.

Top left: The London Hilton Hotel, Park Lane in 1963 – the year it was opened. Accused at the time of violating the London skyline, criticism has diminished since the construction of other tower blocks around Hyde Park. The rooftop bar and restaurant offer spectacular views over the whole of central London. The hotel, which was built by Charles Clore on the site of a row of bomb-damaged Regency houses, rapidly became popular with the new international jet-setters. (Douglas Whitworth)

Above and left: With the Hilton Hotel as a backdrop, these gates at an entrance to Hyde Park were opened by Queen Elizabeth II on 11 July 1993 to honour the Queen Mother. David Wynne designed the exuberant central screen and the gates of patinated stainless steel were designed by Giuseppe Lund.

The Dorchester Hotel, Park Lane in 1948 – an institution since it opened in 1931. The hotel was built on the site of Dorchester House, later Hertford House, which was modelled on the Villa Farnese in Rome. During the war the Dorchester was the headquarters of General Eisenhower, and with its reinforced concrete structure was considered one of the safest buildings in London. The Dorchester's most faithful star visitor has been Elizabeth Taylor. (Douglas Whitworth)

Since the 1948 photograph the tree in the foreground now almost obscures the Dorchester Hotel. Now there are several traffic management changes to be seen. The 'Bobby' on point duty has been replaced by traffic lights, Park Lane is now one-way southbound, and the car in the foreground, traversing a box junction, is about to incur a fixed charge of £8 by entering the London Congestion Zone.

Left: The Duke of Windsor emerging from Lock's the hatters in St James's Street, 1945. After the Duke resigned as Governor of the Bahamas in March 1945 he and the Duchess of Windsor spent some time in America and France before he returned alone to Britain in October of that year, staying with his mother, Queen Mary, at Marlborough House. Lock & Co. was founded in 1676 when Robert Davis opened a hatter's shop at the south-east end of St James's Street. James Lock inherited the business in 1759 and the family connection has continued to the present day. Among the many famous men who have had headgear supplied by Lock's are Lord Nelson and the Duke of Wellington. (Douglas Whitworth)

Below: The social standing of these casually dressed window shoppers cannot compete with Lock's Royal patron – as photographed by Douglas.

Previous page: A Life Guard on duty at Horse Guards, 1953. The two sentries in Whitehall are so much a part of the capital's pageantry that many visitors feel they have not really seen London until they have stood in awe before them. (Douglas Whitworth)

Above left: The Royal Horse Guards (the Blues and Royals) clattering through Hyde Park on their way to Horse Guards in 1949. This is one of the great moments of a London morning when the troop of Horse Guards in their full regalia ride down to Whitehall to perform their guard duties. The Royal Horse Guards were raised by Charles II in 1661 and are distinguished from the Life Guards by their red plumes and blue uniforms. (Douglas Whitworth)

Above right: At about 10.35 a.m. (11.35 a.m. on Sundays) the Blues and Royals take the same route as in the 1949 picture, though now a mounted police officer rides at their head. The 270ft tower block in my photograph is part of the Knightsbridge Barracks, built in 1959.

Left: The traffic is halted as the Horse Guards prepare to cross the 1960s one-way road system before continuing along Constitution Hill. Commissioned by George IV and designed by Decimus Burton in 1825, the Wellington Arch is now open to the public. With three floors of exhibits telling its history and with glorious views from its balconies this must be one of London's best value venues for the visitor.

Top left: A high shot, from the Wellington Arch, of the Royal Horse Guards passing the memorial to the Machine Gun Corps and Royal Artillery. On this cold but bright day they wear red cloaks.

Above right: An immaculate and resplendent Grenadier Guard on duty outside Buckingham Palace in 1953. By the year of the Coronation, full dress uniform was worn on ceremonial occasions. The sentries were then positioned outside the palace railings having no need of protection from the public. (Douglas Whitworth)

Above left: Buckingham Palace Guardsmen, their sentry boxes positioned within the palace grounds, many metres back from the railings, in order to be well away from the disruptive antics of tourists determined to capture a shot for the photo album by posing alongside one of these glamorous figures. A comparatively recently introduced security measure is the armed policeman on duty nearby.

Above: Tourists on the steps of the Queen Victoria Memorial watch the Changing of the Guard in 1948. The Americans in the centre – the man with a Paillard Bolex cine-camera – were among the many visitors from the United States who were arriving in greater numbers. Their affluence was in sharp contrast to that of the British who were still restricted and rationed. The Americans were welcome both for themselves and also for their dollars which were vital to Britain's economy at a time when its balance of payments situation was precarious. (Douglas Whitworth)

Opposite above left: Two smartly uniformed sergeants of the US Marines at ease in Grosvenor Square in 1949. The United States Marine Corps which was founded in 1775 as an arm of the US Navy, man the American embassies throughout the world. In the background are buildings damaged during the war and still awaiting reconstruction. (Douglas Whitworth)

Opposite above right: Three visitors from the provinces pose for the camera at Piccadilly Circus in 1953. Throughout the summer, thousands of people traced the route taken by Queen Elizabeth II after her Coronation. (Douglas Whitworth)

Opposite below: Though many visitors to London have travelled from other parts of the United Kingdom, the majority of groups here to watch the Changing of the Guard seem to be from the Far East. In this digital age a handheld video camera, or even mobile phone, record the ceremony replacing the more cumbersome cine-camera.

Above far left: Broadcasting House in Portland Place, 1949. The headquarters of the BBC opened in 1932 and all the radio programmes, so vital to the morale of the public during the war, were made here. After the end of hostilities the popularity of radio continued with three distinct programmes being provided – the middlebrow Home Service, the popular Light Programme and the highbrow Third Programme. (Douglas Whitworth)

Above left: Eric Gill's sculpture Prospero still gazes out towards Oxford Circus. Although in the 1960s, additional studios and offices were added, the classic view of the original 1930s building appears unchanged.

Left: In 1960 some four miles to the west, on the White City site of the 1908 Franco-British exhibition, the world's first purpose-built television studios, built and equipped to BBC specifications, were opened. I had the pleasure of working on some of the first black and white programmes produced there – colour television was yet to come.

Below left: London in 1953 saw its biggest ever traffic jams. Throughout the summer, cars, buses and coaches carried neck-craning visitors along the Coronation route. Oxford Street particularly drew huge crowds of people bringing traffic to a standstill. Selfridges store, in the background here, was famous for its window displays above which were paintings of famous British characters of the past. (Douglas Whitworth)

Below right: An unusually quiet mid-week Oxford Street as the 'One Man Operator Bus' draws into the bus stop bay. The ticket dispenser in the foreground is a comparative newcomer to London's street furniture. Before entering the bus one must have first bought a ticket from one of these machines (beware no change is given).

For many years on weekdays, Oxford Street has been barred to all vehicles with the exception of buses and taxis and there is a suggestion that the entire length may be pedestrianised with a tram service introduced to provide public transport.

Above left: People strolling on Waterloo Bridge in 1953. The present bridge replaced John Rennie's bridge of 1817 which was considered a masterpiece. In the 1920s a dangerous settlement in the foundations of the pier arches was discovered and a temporary bridge was built in 1925. After a long controversy the old bridge was demolished and although construction of the new bridge began before the war, it was not completed until 1942. Beyond the bridge is the river frontage of Somerset House, then mainly occupied by government offices and now housing the Courtauld Institute Galleries and the Gilbert Collection. (Douglas Whitworth)

Above middle: Saturday morning and Waterloo Bridge is an ideal vantage point to photograph the Millennium Wheel. Cyclists take advantage of the comparative safety of one of the many stretches of cycle lane, while the blue van heads for the Kingsway Tunnel, which surfaces halfway up Kingsway. The attractive backdrop is Somerset House.

Above right and right: Somerset House is now open to the public housing The Courtauld Institute of Art Gallery, the Gilbert Collection and Hermitage Rooms. In the summer the terrace café, overlooking the Thames, is popular, while during the Christmas season Fountain Court is transformed into one of London's most popular venues, a huge skating rink – *the* place to see and be seen.

Above: The *Odelia*, a river launch, passing St Thomas's Hospital in 1953. The hospital was built in 1868-1871 in the continental style with pavilions, and approved by Florence Nightingale who established the Nightingale Training School of Nursing here. To this day the nurses at St Thomas's Hospital are known as 'Nightingales'. Of the seven original pavilions facing the river, only three to the right of the chapel now remain.

The four buildings nearest to Westminster Bridge were severely damaged during the war and were replaced by a 13-storey hospital block. (Douglas Whitworth)

Left: The original 1871 buildings of St Thomas's Hospital, almost hidden now by mature trees. The large white cubic building to the left replaced the four original buildings. The catamaran heading downstream is a regular river service linking Tate Britain and Tate Modern, also stopping at the London Eye. The Tate boat, its exterior and interior designed by artist Damien Hirst, operates a forty-minute service during gallery opening hours.

This is the classic view of the Thames Barrier, the piers marching across the Thames at Woolwich. Work started in 1974, and on 8 May 1984 I had the pleasure of filming the ceremony when the Queen declared the barrier neither open or closed, but 'operational'.

Though the public is not able to visit the control room, a visitor centre details the history and operation of this, arguably, eighth wonder of the world. In the foreground of my shot is a picnic area and children's playgound.

I snatched this, an interesting alternative view of the barrier from the Woolwich Free Ferry. Canary Wharf makes an impressive backdrop and the Millennium Dome can just be made out in the middle distance, empty and still costing the public a small fortune to maintain it until a buyer can be found. The words elephant and white come to mind.

Right: HQS *Wellington*, the Livery Hall of Master Mariners moored by Temple Bar in 1949. The sloop, which was built in Devonport in 1934, served on the New Zealand and China stations before the war, during which she was primarily on convoy escort duties in the North Atlantic. When the *Wellington* was decommissioned by the Admiralty in 1947, the Company of Master Mariners bought the ship and converted it into a floating Livery Hall. (Douglas Whitworth)

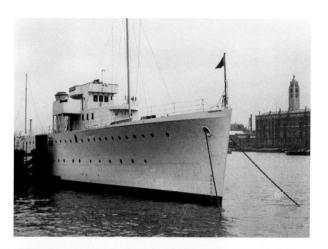

Below: After dark with its illuminated tower reflected in the river – the Oxo Tower. Built as a GPO generating station, it was bought in the 1920s by the Liebig Extract of Meat Co. However, by the late 1970s it had become derelict and likely to be demolished. A 'Save the Oxo Tower', started by a local resident Jane Waller, and taken up by the Coin Street campaign, led to its purchase as one of the 'not for profit' Coin Street Community Buildings' riverside sites. In 1996 with its carefully planned mix of cafés, restaurants, design studios and five floors of social housing, it was opened to the public. On the rooftop, with panoramic views of St Paul's, is the Oxo Tower Restaurant, Bar and Brasserie.

The National Theatre with the evening performance about to start in each of its three auditoriums: with open stage and seating for 1,120, the Olivier. Next in size, with traditional proscenium arch, the Lyttelton. Third, an intimate 300-seat 'studio' space, called the Cottesloe. Easily read from the opposite bank, the illuminated sign marches past, spelling out the theatres' forthcoming productions.

Though the exterior of the National Theatre appears austere, on entering the carpeted interior one immediately feels less intimidated and may browse the titles at the specialist bookshop, attend free exhibitions and music recitals or relax in one of the many bars, cafés and restaurants.

From almost the same camera position, one of a procession of dinner cruises is about to pass under Waterloo Bridge. In the distance can be seen Big Ben and an illuminated Victoria Tower. The London Eye is still doing good business with patrons enjoying a view of London after dark.

Piccadilly Circus in 1948, sparsely decorated for the Olympic Games of that year. Pennants hang from poles on each side of Shaftesbury Avenue and Boots the Chemist have hung a Union Jack outside their shop. There appears to be no traffic control and pedestrians cross the road at all points. The globes on the lamp standards, which were removed during the war, have been replaced but the illuminated advertisements were still not to be lit for another year. (Douglas Whitworth)

The elegant façade of the London Pavilion, much improved after a clean and with all the advertisements removed in 1997, is now renamed the London Trocadero. At a designated crossing point the phased traffic lights ensure a safe crossing for the casually dressed pedestrians. An engineer in high visibility jacket is servicing one set of lights. In the foreground is a motorcycle messenger en route to collect documents for urgent delivery across London.

Piccadilly Circus in 1948. The London Pavilion, with its two façades covered in advertisements, is showing Dick Powell in *To the Ends of the Earth*. A hoarding in Coventry Street advertises the Andrews Sisters at the London Palladium – Hollywood stars who appeared there included Carmen Miranda, Danny Kaye, Bob Hope and Perry Como. Dodging traffic are two men in dark suits, each with an umbrella and both wearing hats, the uniform of the period. (Douglas Whitworth)

The engineer has moved his ladder to service the traffic lights in the centre of this shot. In the foreground the taxi, a TX1, is an example of the first major change in taxi design since 1958 when the FX4, still an Austin product, first took to the roads.

Shaftesbury Avenue, 1959. The street was built in 1886 as part of a slum clearance programme and quickly became London's leading entertainment district with six theatres between Piccadilly Circus and Cambridge Circus. The London Pavilion on the right was opened as a theatre in 1885, and later converted into a cinema. Beyond is the Trocadero Restaurant built in 1896 with its famous Long Bar and advertised at the time as the 'premier restaurant in the world' – it has now been transformed into an entertainment centre. (Douglas Whitworth)

Rising above the curving façade of Shaftesbury Avenue's theatres is Centre Point, a 385ft office block designed by Richard Seifert and built in 1964. None of its office space was released for rent for many years – the subject of much controversy.

At the bottom right-hand corner is a low blue building of utilitarian aspect: the Police Pavilion, where officers are on duty round the clock to provide assistance to the public and as a response centre for any local emergency. The design is based closely on the Police Pavilion in Times Square, Manhattan.

The London Pavilion has been renamed the London Trocadero. Some 'high street' shops remain on the ground floor but escalators to the upper floors are blocked off.

Opposite page, above left: The Empire Cinema in Leicester Square in 1949, built in 1928 on the site of the Empire Theatre. Most films shown in British cinemas were made in Hollywood but the Rank Organisation and Ealing Studios produced distinctive and popular films such as *Maytime in Mayfair*, being shown here, starring Anna Neagle and Michael Wilding. (Douglas Whitworth)

Below left: Dolores Gray and Neville Mapp with the cast of *Annie Get Your Gun* at the Coliseum in 1948. This show, with *Oklahoma!* which was running at the Theatre Royal, Drury Lane at the same time, brought in a new style of musical in which songs were integrated into the plot. *Annie Get Your Gun* ran for 1,147 performances at the Imperial Theatre in New York and the London production ran for four years at the Coliseum. (Douglas Whitworth)

Right: The Royal Opera House, Covent Garden, 1959. Behind the impressive portico and the ornate auditorium the Royal Opera and the Royal Ballet shared cramped backstage facilities until the extensive redevelopments of recent years. The 1950s was the decade when the Bolshoi and Kirov ballet companies made their first celebrated appearances here. Car parking was restricted outside the opera house but cars were apparently allowed to park across the street outside Bow Street Magistrate's Court. (Douglas Whitworth)

This page: Visitors enjoying free musical entertainment at the refurbished Covent Garden Market.

Piccadilly Circus in 1952. The Bovril sign was one of the first illuminated advertisements to appear here in 1910 and others including the Guinness clock became equally famous although *The Times*, in 1928, described the lights as 'a hideous eyesore which no civilised community ought to tolerate'. (Douglas Whitworth)

Since there are no longer any illuminated signs on the London Pavilion, I chose an alternative camera angle, to include the delicately illuminated 'Angel of Christian Charity', universally known, incorrectly, as the 'God of Love' – Eros.

Spot the logo of a British company – I can only identify one, and in the same place as seen in the 1952 photograph – Boots.

The splendid sweep of the Quadrant, the alternative name of this stretch of Regent Street from Piccadilly Circus in 1950. After a century of service, John Nash's elegant buildings were demolished in 1924 and Sir Reginald Blomfield designed this new shopping street. Among the restaurants along this part of Regent Street are the Café Royal – a well-known bohemian haunt – and Veeraswamy, an Indian restaurant famous since the 1920s. (Douglas Whitworth)

Swan & Edgar (to the left of the 1950 picture) the department store where ladies 'up from the home counties' used to shop, is now a Virgin Megastore. Although the western sweep of Regent Street, as it curves to the north, may look unchanged, it is however a huge photo-blow-up concealing major restoration work by the Crown Estate to upgrade this section of the street.

Of the two taxis turning into Regent Street, one remains a traditional black cab while the other, painted in the colours of the company it is paid to advertise, appears rather brash.

Above: Piccadilly Circus in 1953. This awkwardly shaped junction at the heart of London's West End was, after the war, the subject of several redevelopment proposals. Most involved demolishing the north-east section of the Circus, replacing it with tower blocks but fortunately none of them were implemented. The Circus may not be the most beautiful sight in London but it remains a popular venue for millions of tourists each year. (Douglas Whitworth)

Left: No great change in this view of Piccadilly Circus from Douglas' 1953 shot, though the façade of the London Pavilion is improved – now free of its neon signs. Also Eros is no longer on an island site after changes in traffic flow. In the centre of the shot, the red London bus is one of the few remaining Routemaster buses kept in service and operating on two heritage routes.

Above left: A news vendor selling the *Evening News* in Piccadilly, 1953. There were then three evening papers published in London – the *Evening News*, associated with the *Daily Mail*, the *Evening Standard* from Lord Beaverbrook's Express group and the *Star* published by the *News Chronicle*. Invariably these would be sold by news vendors standing only yards apart although some newspaper sellers would handle all three titles and their cry 'News, Star, Standard!' was quite familiar. (Douglas Whitworth)

Above right: Offering the only evening newspaper still for sale (there is currently a war between competing free newspapers) our news vendor has some protection from the weather. He sells the *Evening Standard* from a lightweight stand with its placards proclaiming the latest 'hot' news story. In the foreground, a lady offers a small flower to two innocent young visitors to the city. Just visible, the top of an historic relic from the past – a blue police post rendered obsolete by police two-way radio.

Below left: American tourists are among the pedestrians crossing Shaftesbury Avenue in 1953. London in the weeks preceding the Coronation of Queen Elizabeth II was crowded with visitors, particularly from America, and hotel rooms were at a premium. Frank's Barber Shop on the left has been a well-known feature of Piccadilly Circus since 1911. (Douglas Whitworth)

Below right: An accredited tour guide leads a small group for a visit to St Paul's Cathedral. Tourists now dress for comfort – T-shirts and loose fitting slacks are the order of the day (not a skirt in sight). And for foot comfort when pounding the tourist trail, the footwear of choice is a pair of trainers.

Top left: Visitors relax in Leicester Square away from the crowded streets of the West End a few days before the Coronation of Queen Elizabeth II in 1953. The Empire Cinema, with its panoramic screen is topically showing *Young Bess* starring Jean Simmons, Stewart Grainger, Deborah Kerr and Charles Laughton. The Monseigneur News Theatre programme typically lasted an hour and included two newsreels, cartoons and a short topical film. (Douglas Whitworth)

Middle left: The Empire Cinema. The huge area where the current programme was spelled out, with 'use again' letters, has been removed to reveal the buildings attractive façade. The replacement canopy is also an improvement. I arrived as a team was at work putting in place the billboard, designed and produced to promote the current programme.

Bottom left: Coventry Street in 1948. The Victorian Queens House on the right is a bar and the Monseigneur News Theatre is showing the latest newsreels of the Olympic Games then being held in the capital. The adjoining Empire Cinema is presenting Judy Garland and Gene Kelly in *The Pirate*. (Douglas Whitworth)

Bottom right: The road to the north of Leicester Square together with parts of Coventry Street is now pedestrianised. Social changes over the last fifty years are nicely illustrated by the changes in usage of The Monseigneur News Theatre – a casino, and the Queens House – now a branch of the American Starbucks chain of coffee houses. Behind the Paramedic car, cycle and motorcycle rapid response paramedics are standing by for the next emergency call. In the middle distance is the Empire Cinema.

The National Gallery and St Martin-in-the-Fields in 1953. On the left, in front of the National Gallery, scaffolding is being erected to hold the viewing stands being built on the processional route for the forthcoming Coronation. (Douglas Whitworth)

In spite of taxi drivers' dire warnings of traffic chaos if the road in front of the National Gallery was closed to traffic, the pedestrianisation went ahead and without the predicted traffic jams.

The new accessibility of Trafalgar Square has proved to be a popular measure with tourists, lunchtime locals and the feral pigeons. Although the resident bird-food sellers have been banned from the square, well-meaning but misguided 'amateurs' still turn up to feed them. Flocks of the birds have migrated to this new pedestrian area in front of the National Gallery. There to photograph the National Gallery, as I pressed the shutter release of my camera, a sudden noise alarmed the pigeons and I found myself in a blizzard of birds – Alfred Hitchcock would have been proud of me.

A sunny afternoon in Trafalgar Square in 1953. The glorious church of St-Martin-in-the-Fields, the model for many other churches, especially in America, has a long tradition of caring for the homeless and unfortunate. For years now, Trafalgar Square had been the traditional site of social and political meetings. In 1996 Nelson Mandela addressed thousands of people from the balcony of South Africa House, just to the right of the photograph. (Douglas Whitworth)

Above left: Although in fifty-three years this scene had remained unchanged, I have included this shot because it looks even better in colour. The young lady photographing her friend by the fountain agrees.

Above middle: Looking north from Whitehall, Nelson's Column dominates Trafalgar Square. It is seen here in mid-July 2006, shortly before scaffolding is removed after a major four-month restoration (the last clean was twenty years ago). The column was erected in 1843 and over the years there have been many guesses as to its height. During this restoration – using laser technology – it was possible to arrive at the accurate figure of 169ft, topped by Nelson's statue at an additional 17ft.

Above right: Taking the last opportunity to film from the top of the column, this close-up shot shows a news presenter and his crew at work.

Right: Nelson's Column from Admiralty Arch after cleaning and restoration work was completed.

Left: The Bank of England in 1951. The windowless (for security) ground floor was designed by Sir John Soane in 1833 – the massive block rising above was the work of Sir Herbert Baker in the 1920s. The figure of the 'Old Lady of Threadneedle Street' appears in the pediment. On the right, behind the equestrian statue of the Duke of Wellington is the Royal Exchange, although no exchange business is now transacted there. With the nearby Mansion House, these two buildings remain relics of an age which preferred classical porticos and are now dwarfed by the city's tower blocks. In an air raid on 12 January 1944 Bank Station, under this intersection, took a direct hit with great loss of life and creating a huge crater in the road. (Douglas Whitworth)

Bottom left: The exteriors of the Bank of England and the Royal Exchange, although cleaned, are unchanged. In 1988, some of Soane's original designs were included when the Bank of England's interior was converted into a museum, illustrating its changing role from its foundation in 1694 to the present day as the UK's central bank. Beyond, high-rise development continues.

Crossing the box junction is one of the latest designs of a 'one-man operator' bus, a replacement for the popular Routemaster.

In the right foreground is one of the growing band of commuters who have discovered the motorcycle or motor scooter as the ideal vehicle for their daily commute. For others, a potent symbol of worldly success is the ownership of a 'weekend motorcycle', either the latest and hugely powerful Japanese model or a brutal American Harley Davidson.

Opposite: Almost four centuries separate the foreground and the backdrop of this photograph. The Queens House was built in the grounds of Greenwich Park in the early part of the seventeenth century, while Canary Wharf is a late twentieth-century development.

Following the closure of the loss-making PLA West India and Millwall Docks, between 1978 and 1980, the Docklands Development Corporation was created to 'Secure regeneration by encouraging industry and commerce, encourage people to live and work in the area by providing housing and social facilities.'

In 1991 the first tenant moved into Canary Wharf, the highest tower in London and the developer's flagship project. With the resurgence of confidence after a period of severe recession, work started on twin towers (to right of Canary Wharf); both were ready for occupation in late 2001, by HSBC and Citigroup Banks. The cranes seen here are likely to be working well into the twenty-first century.

Lunch time at Canary Wharf and some of the 80,000 people working at the Canary Wharf Estate, leave their offices. Some relax in one of the landscaped gardens surrounding the main offices or lunch at one of the many cafés, bars and restaurants.

A Docklands Light Railway train leaves Canary Wharf Station. The key to the success of Canary Wharf was good communication with central London.

1987 The Docklands Light Railway opened.

1991 Extended to connect with the underground network at Bank Station.

1999 Canary Wharf Station on the Jubilee Line was operational.

2005 DLR link to London City Airport opened.

2010 A further extension to Stratford International and the Eurostar service.

Above left: Many of the West India Import Dock warehouses have been preserved, their interiors remodelled as shops and restaurants. One is now the Docklands Museum, partner of the Museum of London. It has three floors of exhibits, many interactive, and celebrates the history of the Thames and the importance of London's docks to the nation.

Above right: A cargo boat tied up at London Bridge Wharf in 1948. This was still the heyday of the Port of London, despite the considerable damage to the docks and warehouses caused during the Blitz of the Second World War. Many visitors to London were unaware of the scale of the docks, which had forty-five miles of quays. Between 1967 and 1981 all the great docks closed, victim of new cargo-handling techniques at the container ports of Tilbury and Felixstowe. The London Docklands Development Corporation was set up to administer the changes as grim warehouses gave way to modern office blocks and apartments. The warehouse in the background here was demolished and replaced by Sugar Quay, a modern block of apartments. (Douglas Whitworth)

Right: Tower Bridge opens to allow the *Silver Cloud*, a comparatively small though luxuriously appointed, cruise liner to tie up alongside HMS *Belfast*. *Silver Cloud* is about to embark on an eleven-day cruise of the Bay of Biscay. Passing, is the Harbour Master's launch.

The Notting Hill Carnival took to the streets of West London in 1965 and is the largest street festival in Europe. Caribbean in flavour, it attracts young people from across the world determined to be part of the 500,000 who attend the parade on each of the two days (Sunday and Monday) of the August Bank Holiday. It takes several hours for the steel bands, accompanied by their exotically dressed dancers, to complete the route. Red snapper and goat curry are among the Caribbean delicacies on offer from stalls along the entire route, by vendors, many of whom came to England in the 1950s. (This year I sampled Bajan fish cake and a Banks, the beer of Barbados.)

Celebrating the October Moon, in the streets north of Leicester Square, shoppers come to the doors of Chinese supermarkets and diners at noodles bars put aside their chopsticks to watch the Dragon Dancers as they parade through London's China Town.

A small cargo boat sailing under Tower Bridge in 1947. In as short a time as a minute the 1,200-ton arms of the bridge can be raised to allow a ship through. This happened 655 times in the first month of its operation in 1894 but now the bridge is opened on average only forty times a month. When the bridge was the gateway to London and the Pool was crowded with shipping, a tug was kept riding at anchor, but with steam up, to be of assistance to a ship in difficulties and endangering the bridge. (Douglas Whitworth)

The sun is almost always in the wrong position for successful photography from the North Bank. As a walkway lined with restaurants and bars has also been opened up on the South Bank I cheated by crossing the river for my shot of the bascules closing behind sailing barge *May*. A bonus to this camera position is the view between the two towers, which includes both Tower 42 and the Swiss Re Tower. The hydraulically operated bascules were converted from steam power to electrical in 1976.

Above: On her way to join other Thames sailing barges at her berth in the West Basin, *May* passes the Ivory House, now converted into shops, restaurants and apartments.

Above right: Sailing barge *May* leaving the Thames by St Katherine's Dock lock. Completed in 1827, St Katherine's Dock was the last of London's docks to be built – also the first to close. It is now a popular tourist venue.

Below right: The Grand Vista at the Festival Pleasure Gardens at Battersea, 1951. This was the lighter side of the Festival of Britain promising entertainment and relaxation for everyone. Within the gardens were open-air cafés, an amusement park, a children's zoo, illuminations and fireworks. Some of the features in the gardens remained after the festival year and a major restoration followed. (Douglas Whitworth)

Above: A new focal point to the north of the park, overlooking the river, is the 100ft-high Peace Pagoda built by Buddhist monks in 1985 to commemorate Hiroshima Day.

Top right: In mid-2000 work started to restore an area, previously occupied by the Festival Pleasure Gardens, which over the years had been allowed to gently decay. The fountains and the associated walkways have been restored to their 1951 glory and are once again looking delightfully 'Festival of Britain'.

Bottom right: By a happy accident my visit to photograph the Peace Pagoda was on a Bank Holiday when, across the park all the traditional rides and sideshows of Carter's Steam Fair were attracting large crowds. In the background of the chair-o-plane ride, a lovingly restored traction engine kept 'steam up' to supply the 110 volts to some of the rides.

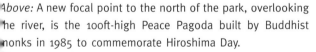

73

Above: I was leaving Battersea Park after photographing the fun fair, with all its noise and frenetic activity, when I came across this delightfully peaceful scene – what a contrast.

Opposite: Relaxing in Hyde Park in 1952. Hyde Park has been a place of relaxation and fashion since the sixteenth century and together with adjoining Kensington Gardens forms the largest park in central London. (Douglas Whitworth)

Road menders at Hyde Park Corner in 1950. Workmen are asphalting the road surface with hot tar and stone chippings. In those days this task was performed manually, the tar being carried from the flaming cauldron in wheelbarrows and spread evenly over the road. (Douglas Whitworth)

Left: Bayswater Road closed to traffic as workmen repair yet another ruptured water main.

In the 1950s photographs work on London's roads depended on muscle power; now the big yellow machines have taken the strain. A flat cap, stout pair of boots and possibly a bib and brace were the accepted wear on all building and civil engineering sites. Now placards proclaim that, to work on this site a high-visibility jacket, protective footwear, safety helmet and, under certain circumstances, ear protection and safety goggles are mandatory.

Opposite: Sunlight streams in Liverpool Street Station in 1946. The station was one of the sights of London, despite having suffered considerable damage during the Blitz. The Gothic tower, which surmounted the entrance, was destroyed along with much of the buildings façade. The station was built by the Great Eastern Railway Co. in 1874 on the site of Bethlem Royal Hospital, known as Bedlam, and quickly became London's busiest terminal. The forward-looking plans drawn up after the war for modernisation of the station, including a helicopter landing pad on the roof, never materialised. Liverpool Street Station has now been incorporated into the Broadgate complex with an amphitheatre and piazzas. (Douglas Whitworth)

Opposite page, left: Here at Liverpool Street Station the impossibility of recreating the wonderful atmosphere of Douglas' taxi rank was immediately obvious – both trains and passengers no longer smoke. However, the recently cleaned Victorian brickwork and in particular, the beautifully designed ironwork, was well worth recording. Several designs of London taxi are on the rank, last in line and the latest design – a TX11.

Above right: Unheard of when Douglas took his shot – a female taxi driver. When I photographed Alex in her smart golden cab with its personalised number plate ALX she was just leaving the rank with a fare, but had time to tell me that she got 'the Knowledge' five years ago.

Below right: A fine example of a vintage 50s FX3 taking part in a parade of vintage cars on its way to Buckingham Palace in 2006.

This page: Two Scots Guardsmen feeding the pigeons in Trafalgar Square in 1949. (Douglas Whitworth)

The Strand in the rain in 1948 from the entrance of Moon's Garage. Across the street, as busy then as it is today, are Mooney's Irish Bar, Slaters restaurant and Marjorie Moores Marriage Bureau, this being one of few such agencies in London at the time. The Strand, famous for the Savoy Hotel and Simpson's Restaurant, was also a street of specialist shops and businesses, including stamp dealers. (Douglas Whitworth)

None of the buildings in the 1948 shot have survived a substantial redevelopment of the Strand, apart from a few notable exceptions including the Savoy Hotel and the Coal Hole pub. The Strand has become rather bland, so I chose an alternative 'rainy day' location, Jermyn Street, where gentlemen choose to shop. Across the street Hackett the tailors and outfitters, John Lobb for handmade shoes and Floris selling their own brand of fragrances, are a few examples of the street's fashionable shops.

Top left: Police Officers patrolling Leicester Square. Now, both male and female officers carry out exactly the same duties and face the same challenges. Both officers are wearing anti-stab vests and carry, as a replacement for the traditional truncheon, a police baton. Handcuffs. a CS canister and two-way radio complete their accoutrement.

Top right: Community Support Officers patrolling Oxford Street, first introduced in 2002. Although wearing a uniform similar to Police Officers, their powers are restricted and they have no power of arrest. Their main function, in addition to being the Met's eyes and ears on London's streets, is to provide additional security for the public.

Bottom left: A paramedic in Leicester Square, an ideal central location for a rapid response to medical emergencies in the West End. It is a sad fact that his olive-green jacket has to be made of stab-proof material.

Bottom middle and right: Speedier transport for the paramedics through heavy and slow moving traffic is the cycle paramedic. He wears a high-visibility jacket and the four panniers on his yellow cycle contain all the necessary equipment, including oxygen and a defibrillator for his front-line duties. The motorcycle paramedic is similarly equipped.

Far right: Derby County supporters in front of Buckingham Palace in 1946. The fans, with their rosettes and rattles, took in the sights of London before making their way to Wembley Stadium for the cup final against Charlton Athletic. The Derby fans went home happy with their team winning 4-1 after extra time. (Douglas Whitworth)

Above right: Part of a crowd of 54,000 'Gunners' fans on their way to support Arsenal for the first game to be played at its just completed Emirates Stadium. This first game, Arsenal v Ajax, was a testimonial in honour of popular Arsenal player Dennis Bergkamp.

Below right: The huge crowd of Arsenal supporters were well-behaved but the joyful spirit of the Derby County supporters, in Douglas' photo, seemed to me entirely absent. The Emirates Stadium, built at a cost of £390 million, replaced the much loved, but ageing home to the 'Gunners'. It is hoped that as part of the redevelopment of the old Highbury Stadium site, the front elevation, a 1920s architectural icon, will be preserved. At the final whistle – the score Arsenal 2 Ajax 1.

Top left: A motorcycle speedway meeting at Harringay in 1948. Speedway was very popular in the early post-war years and attendances were high. Harringay raced against Wembley at this meeting and the Harringay captain Vic Duggan, an Australian, and his opposite number Bill Kitchen, were well-known for their friendly but competitive rivalry. (Douglas Whitworth)

Above: The Olympic Games at Wembley Stadium, 1948. These were called the austerity Olympics as no new stadiums were built for the events and there was little ostentation. London was given the games without any opposition but British athletes were not very successful, winning no gold medals. The athletic events at Wembley were very well-attended – this race was a 400m heat won by the Jamaican Arthur Wint who went on to win the final. These games were the first to be televised although coverage was only in the London area and very few television receivers were then in use. (Douglas Whitworth)

Left: The 2012 Olympics are to be held at a purpose-built site in East London; with costs spiralling and construction work at too early a stage for photography there is no chance for me to update Douglas' 1948 historic Olympic Games picture.

Here at Wembley, the traditional venue for the cup final, construction workers are still on site. Plagued by delays and so far costing £800 million, it is due to open in May 2007.

Left and below left: With the Albert Memorial in the background, 30,000 joggers gather in Hyde Park for the annual Run London race.

Below and below right: After signalling the official start of this 10km race, Olympic medal winners, Paula Radcliffe representing North London (green T-shirt) and Sebastian Coe, South London (yellow T-shirt) joined the runners. The winner was Chris Thompson in 30 minutes 4 seconds.

Above left: An orator at Speakers' Corner near Marble Arch, 1949. The speaker seems determined to read from his sermons although the attention of his audience appears to be elsewhere. The right to hold assemblies here was granted in 1872 after a series of angry demonstrations, but police retain full jurisdiction over the speakers. (Douglas Whitworth)

Above right: A speaker at Marble Arch in 1949 who appears to be deriving some amusement from his audience. Orators at this famous spot include extremists, eccentrics and the most earnest of religious speakers, each with a circle of listeners. (Douglas Whitworth)

Left: A button-holed speaker in Hyde Park with oversized pages of religious tracts in 1949. This well-dressed man in pin-striped trousers is well-prepared with a ladder giving him an advantage over his audience. Most speakers seem to enjoy the cut-and-thrust of the exchanges even though listeners may be unconvinced by the orators' messages. (Douglas Whitworth)

Large crowds are still drawn to listen to the orators, who return each Sunday to proclaim their message. Now, the firebrand political activists seem to have been overtaken by those with strong religious beliefs.

Left: A street trader in full flow at Petticoat Lane market, 1949. The street, which was renamed Middlesex Street in the nineteenth century, besides being a market where clothes can be bought has all manner of bric-a-brac for sale. In the years immediately after the war when goods were in short supply, this market served a useful purpose. (Douglas Whitworth)

Below top left: Ras Prince Monolulu sells horse-racing tips to onlookers, in Petticoat Lane in 1949. The 'prince' was a familiar figure at racecourses and elsewhere before and after the war, in full warrior dress with huge multi-coloured ostrich feathers on his head. He sold his race selections at a nominal 6d or 1s each, and although the horse may not have won, it was worth the money merely to talk to him. His cry, 'I've got a horse', became famous, but this giant of a man could draw a crowd by his appearance alone. (Douglas Whitworth)

Below bottom left: A couple listening to a salesman in Petticoat Lane, 1949. (Douglas Whitworth)

Below right: A persuasive salesman in Petticoat Lane in 1950. Stallholders often show a ready wit but will also take advantage of customers searching for a bargain. The modern market has now spread into the surrounding streets, each with its own character. (Douglas Whitworth)

Saturday is market day in Portobello Road. Tourists from around the world are drawn to the most famous of all street markets. With over a mile of trader's stalls one can start at Notting Hill to browse the antique stalls, buy some fruit and vegetables, or feast at one of the many fast-food stalls before reaching the bric-a-brac stalls at Ladbroke Grove. Even then if you get lost or confused there's always a friendly London 'Bobby' to help.

Opposite: All the traffic and visitors headed for The Mall in the Coronation year of 1953. This graceful arch – one of four – spanned the processional way leading to Buckingham Palace. The arches, surmounted by two golden lions and two white unicorns, supported a Princess's coronet and were floodlit at night. Stands for spectators lined the whole of The Mall and in front of the palace – these were fully occupied hours before the Coronation procession was due. Cars in The Mall here include a Ford V8 Pilot on the right, behind which is a Standard Vanguard and retreating on the left is a Ford 8, sporting a rear luggage rack. (Douglas Whitworth)

Above left: Old Bond Street splendidly decorated for the Coronation in 1953. Most streets in the West End were garlanded. On the right is Scott's the hatters, with the royal coat of arms above the doorway. Scott's was founded in the 1870s taking over from an outfitters which had been in existence since 1758. This was one of the few businesses in London still delivering goods by horse and carriage, with the driver and his companion both dressed in a uniform and top hat. In the early 1970s Scott amalgamated with Lock's of St James's Street and this shop was then closed. (Douglas Whitworth)

Above right: The flags are out throughout the length of The Mall and pedal cycles, the only vehicles permitted.

Right: On an afternoon in June 2006, as part of Queen Elizabeth's official eightieth birthday celebrations, a parade of eighty British cars (one from each year of the Queen's life) circle the Victoria Monument before entering and parking in Buckingham Palace grounds, each car displaying its year of manufacture. Appropriately, the first took to the road in 1926.

Above left: Oxford Street from the Cumberland Hotel in 1950. Shoppers and strollers cross the sunny road, half of which is being resurfaced. The east-bound traffic has been re-routed adding to the road problems of this part of London. A barrow boy has taken advantage of the partial road closure to site his stall on the roadway. The south and shady side of Oxford Street never possessed any great department stores but the north side boasted Selfridges, John Lewis, Marshall & Snelgrove, Bourne & Hollingsworth and D.H. Evans. (Douglas Whitworth)

Above right: On the right are a spectacular array of hats in C&A Modes shop window on Oxford Street in 1949. This vast store, then one of the major attractions for shoppers at Marble Arch had numerous floors and departments. These stylish hats, copies of the latest Parisian models perhaps, ranged in price from 7s 6d to 35s 6d. (Douglas Whitworth)

Right: Shop window-gazers at Dolcis shoe shop on Oxford Street in 1949. (Douglas Whitworth)

Left: While many of our High Street shops have disappeared, this tranquil Victorian arcade, between Piccadilly and Jermyn Street, continues to prosper and becomes evermore exclusive.

Below left: On a busy road out of London this glass palace to successful merchandising is one of the thriving supermarkets boasting twenty-four-hour opening.

Below right: The owner of this Chinese take-away awaits the next customer for his speciality Peking Crispy Fried Duck. Chinese and Indian food is now a staple part of our diet and a wide variety of fast-food takeaway restaurants proliferate.

Far left above: The demolition gang have already started to nibble at one corner of the annexe to County Hall. Built on an island site at the southern end of Westminster Bridge, it has been voted London's most hated building. It's finally going. In the foreground is the Duck Bus, giving its passengers views of London from both land and water.

Far left below: The last of Kensington's great department stores has just closed. First to go – the venerable Pontings, then Derry and Toms, after a short renaissance as the trendy Biba, and finally the dear departed – Barker's.

Left: With the introduction of parking ticket-dispensing machines, parking meters are disappearing from London's streets. Those few meters still standing guard over vacant parking bays in the Congestion Zone have been commandeered by the new breed of cycling commuter, as convenient posts to chain their bikes.

Below left: A winter afternoon – the tug *Mersina* has just passed under Blackfriars Bridge, its destination the landfill site at Mucking on the Thames Estuary. Each day, an hour before high tide, *Mersina* leaves Wandsworth towing two barges laden with containers of domestic and industrial waste. The same journey is made by tugs from other London boroughs and is now the only regular commercial traffic to be seen on the Thames.

Below right: A tug in the Pool of London in 1949 – one of the hundreds then operating on the River Thames. The warehouses on the far south bank of the Thames have all now been demolished to be replaced by the new Greater London Assembly Building. (Douglas Whitworth)

Right: One of the finest views in London – the scene from the bridge over the lake in St James's Park, 1953. The crowded domes and spires of Whitehall resemble the Kremlin or an oriental palace when seen here from London's oldest park. There are, in fact, three great buildings in view – Horse Guards, the domed War Office and the roof of the National Liberal Club. (Douglas Whitworth)

Below: The River Thames at Chiswick, Barnes and Putney Bridge. Away from the bustle of the city the river remains a tranquil playground for leisure and sailing. The scullers are out whatever the weather.

Left: The return of London's lights in 1945. The blackout of windows ended on 23 April, but so many homes switched on their lights in celebration that they caused power failures. Street lighting remained switched off until 25 July to give electricians time to restore the lamps. These American soldiers, and a girlfriend, admire the lights near City Road. (Douglas Whitworth)

Right: Derby County supporters survey the blitzed areas around St Paul's Cathedral on 27 April 1946. From early in the morning, football fans had poured into London for the cup final between Derby County and Charlton Athletic, the first one since the war. Derby County won the match. (Douglas Whitworth)